The Sound of a Collective Pulse

The Sound of a Collective Pulse

Poems by

Cristina M. R. Norcross

Cover design by Shay Culligan
Cover photo by Chris Charles on Unsplash

ISBN: 978-1-63980-021-6

Kelsay Books
502 South 1040 East, A-119
American Fork, Utah 84003
Kelsaybooks.com

This book is dedicated to our shared humanity, our deep connections, and the strength of the human spirit during the pandemic times of 2020.

Acknowledgments

I would like to extend a special thank you to the literary magazines, journals, and anthologies where some of the poems from *The Sound of a Collective Pulse* were first published.

As Above So Below: "Crossing Invisible Lines," "The No Name Time"

An Ariel Anthology Vol. 6: "What the Trees Remember"

Beat Generation: "Closing Time"

The Ekphrastic Review: "The Blue Meadow," "Percolation," "To Celebrate the Bountiful"

Poetry Hall: "The Sound of a Collective Pulse"

Trees in a Garden of Ashes—Poetry of Resilience: "River Source of Strength"

Through This Door—Wisconsin in Poems: "New Dimensions"

Verse-Virtual: "Naked Selves," "We Stitch Ourselves Together"

Visual Verse: "Blueprints for Tomorrow," "The Last Drop of Water," "Leaping Over Unknown Waters," "Leave the Light On," "A Mind Filled with Stars," "The Quiet Hum of Existence," "A Safe Place to Breathe," "Sitting with Wonder," "We Breathe the Same Air"

The Weekly Avocet: "The Earth's Resting Heartbeat"

Contents

New Dimensions

This winter heart you carry
longs to trace the outline of a wing.
Open yourself.
Unfurl, like petals longing to bloom.
New worlds await
behind that door—
that beaded curtain.
You are the opening
to the next dimension.
Color breathes here—
hues of chalcedony blue
and stargazer violet.
Whatever your flickering heart
can imagine—
it lives.
Let go of unwanted burdens.
Wings will appear—
transparent, gold dust flutterings.
Your heartbeat pulses
to the rhythm of a new atmosphere.
You are building a new world—
where the sky is moss green,
jasper stones vibrate beneath your feet,
and all who open the door
are welcome.

Leaping Over Unknown Waters

(Inspired by an image by Andi Sapey and Other.Dance.Art)

Humans long to fly,
suspended over the earth,
unfettered by its strong pull of gravity.
The artist's mind propels itself
above cloud cover,
around jagged rocks,
and through narrow pathways.
To paint, to write, to make music
on a blank canvas
is to fashion new worlds
out of the thinnest air.
The dancer's body
is a clever instrument.
Muscled limbs become a scissor kick in the wind,
an open-angled warrior pose,
the leaping over unknown waters
with a wide-open heart.
Unnatural feats live inside the
arms and legs of the dancer.
She sees beyond the confines of body.
He knows the freedom
that only movement brings—
movement out of the old ways of seeing
and being.
Point to where you need to be
and make the grand jeté.
to the other side.

Little Sparks of Gold

Whatever you think you may have lost,
you haven't.
Your bones still question things.
Your feet feel the low rumble of uncertainty.
Your mouth forms curious shapes,
whispers the sun's urgent bidding,
and becomes the bursting bloom
of all things gloriously honest.
Speak your singing truth
to the sky.
Live the little sparks of gold.

Blueprints for Tomorrow

(Inspired by an image by John Samuel Pughe)

Our burdened earth feels complicated
and precarious, so we imagine wings,
boats that can fly, and blimps
that can whisk us away
to higher altitudes.
Are viruses afraid of heights?
2020 has been an out of body experience.
It is no surprise that the collective dream
is to hang glide and float.
The air up there must be better,
loftier, decorated with scattered clouds
and the occasional, bold bird.

Looking above means choosing to hope,
searching for answers, and allowing the mind
to follow a footpath into the future,
as if promise lives there.

The old ways of being and thinking,
like outdated modes of transportation,
must be let go.
We begin to drop doubt,
like handfuls of grain in a field.
Blueprints for tomorrow
are sketched today
by artists, scientists, and thinkers.
Steady hands draw lines and angles,
erase first drafts and start over.
Ideas keep rising, flapping in earnest
just to stay propelled in the air.
Despite the gravitational pull
to do nothing,
humans keep attempting to fly.

The Earth's Resting Heartbeat

Mornings tinged with gold,
like rolled oats and honey,
now greet me with the coolness
of lake rocks.
Fall brings the hint of subtle change.
Open meadows once bright with dew
become a silent, still green,
awaiting the slow growth and dormancy
of winter.

All living things bow their heads
in prayerful gratitude for the flow of days.
Rippled water at the shore
no longer feels the push and pull
of boat engines.
Tall stalks with blooms reaching for the sun
will soon sleep and wait for spring's renewal.
Like blankets pulled up to chins,
nature's coverings will soon prepare
for autumn's evening calm—curtains being drawn.
The earth's resting heartbeat state
is a deep slumber for us all.

Naked Selves

Thoughts are bones,
long femurs waking us home
to the self.
Our mouths speak smoke signals.
We call out to the universe
in earnest.
Raindrops fall,
tapping us awake.
We enter the space of awareness.
Words shared are medicine—
salve,
balm,
and bandage.
Each vowel rises to the ceiling,
then falls.
Our minds are porous,
drinking in every last nuance.
What was once a dream
of how life could be
becomes embedded in the skin.
It sings songs of acceptance.
Together, we wonder at our very existence,
dancing with our truest, naked selves.
We are not alone.

The Sound of a Collective Pulse

The news comes on—
a stream of lightning bolt events.
We feel the jolt of loss and destruction
speed through the spine
and every connected bone.
This is what it means to ache.

After five months of carefully navigating
an unsure world,
nothing feels the same.
We cannot touch. We stand far apart.
Home feels safer.
This is what it means to fear the invisible foe.

We connect through voice, word, and video.
We learn to make time,
because all we have is time.
We learn to stand still
and drink in the vast expanse
of unscheduled hours.
This is what it means to exist.

We sit together and feel the sky burst
inside our chests.
We listen to the sound
of a collective pulse.
This is what it means to hope.

The Blue Meadow

(Inspired by Tower of Blue Horses by Franz Marc)

Four horses started appearing in our back field, like blue ghosts.
They would follow each other and pause to graze, their heads
quietly bowing as if in prayer. They kissed me with their eyes
every time they looked up, little stars emanating from their manes
and finding my cheek. The blue of the sky seemed to match the
blue of their smooth, shining coats, but I knew that this was
impossible. My vision must have blurred, or perhaps I was seeing
their aura of cobalt purpose and authentic voice. I brought my
morning tea with me and a book to read, just to be close to their
essence of freedom and gliding movements. Soon, their collective
muse energy inspired writing, and every poem was infused with a
spectrum of blue. I wrote about blue jays, cornflowers, the wide
cerulean sea, the melancholy moods of winter mornings, and the
hopefulness of cloudless, robin's egg skies. Blue now lived inside
of me. So did the stars from my cheeks. I walked with feet that
knew the salt of the ocean. My hair swayed in the wind as if lifted
by wings. I took time to pause and listen to my heart's morning
song. The meadow only emptied of all things blue, when my pages
were filled. For weeks after the horses left, I could still hear their
hoofbeats. I could still smell the scent of cornflowers. Anticipation
is my companion. I now wait for mandalas of color to gallop to my
door.

River Source of Strength

Knowing eyes
contain the warmth of
summer's sun-kissed rays
and the patience of endless days.
This was my grandmother's all-embracing grace,
bestowed with each,
gentle cradle of my palm.
Stories of family
emerged on her tongue,
as she held my hand.
History passed from skin to skin this way.
She spoke of the island of her ancestors,
goats clinging to cliffs,
and the persistence of the people
who made a life there.
She brought this steadfast devotion
with her to the mainland.
It followed her every movement,
like a feather of smoke—
from the job she earned
based on her ability to sew a special button,
to her brave first steps
after having a stroke.
To find courage at every new beginning
is the great river source of strength.

Sitting with Wonder

Black pearl eyes look out onto the world
with wonder.
The canvas captures this early you.
Only twelve at the time,
I wish I could have told you then
that the good days will outweigh
the bad, that feeling shadow moments
will make you stronger.

On the day of the portrait,
an unsettled, can't sit still feeling
fills the room.
Seeing the paints co-mingle on the palette,
in a sea of color spectrum swirls,
provides the comfort of things
that meld together and form something new.
I remember sinking into the chair
and feeling more at ease.

Each day we begin anew,
recreate the tender self,
move through the world
with a knowing sense
of how we fill space and time.

How to Risk One Moment

It comes in tidal waves of feeling.
The somersault of the stomach,
the sweat while sleeping,
the breath that never seems
quite deep enough.
Let the waves carry us
instead of sweeping us
into a sandy crash landing.
We will no longer be fighting ourselves.
The small things we can do live inside the chest
and dance in the feet.
We can hold hands with fear,
softly touching fragile leaves on a tree.
Unknowns become knowable,
eventually.
Risk one moment,
then bravely step forward
for the next one.
Courage comes in complex, small pieces.
Nothing is overcome all at once.

Percolation

(Inspired by Nighthawks by Edward Hopper)

Conversations percolate,
much like coffee, around here.
The clinking of cheap mugs
and the scraping of forks on egg-stained plates
is actually a symphony in my head.
Words, nuances, and glances swirl around me.
At this counter, I am witness to
the early morning steam of thought,
the grinding gears of colleagues deep in discussion,
much like the coffee beans whirling in the grinder.
It is nothing short of glorious.
I am not watching the world walk by—
I am welcoming human interaction,
in all of its cacophony of sound and splendor.

Rachel recently separated from her husband.
She comes here after pottery class every Thursday night,
ordering a small slice of lemon meringue pie
and a mint tea.
I love hearing her stories of creation and color.
The counter comes to life,
when envisioning the sloping curves of a vase.

Trent and his chess mates come here after school.
They can only afford a Coke,
but I spot them some chips.
We buy them in bulk.
Kids are good at sharing.
Their laughter bubbles
and echoes from every corner of this joint.
We are renewed by the joy of youth—
find solace in making things, like pie and pottery.
We share counter space.

Uncertain Feet

We are living in the now time
of uncertain feet
and tissue paper plans.
To see beyond requires a willingness
to hold the railing,
when we don't know where
the stairs lead.
So, we stand 6 feet apart,
take comfort in the small things
we can share,
like the recipe for lentil soup
or a photo of wildflowers
on our morning walk.
How odd to move forward
when it feels like
we're on a bridge to nowhere.
The secret is simply to move
every day and remember how
our hands once connected in greeting.
We will touch palms again.

What the Trees Remember

Branches reach for each other
with trembling hands,
like separated lovers.

How long it has been, you say.
How far away you seem—
even across this narrow stream.
Miles and miles—
there is only split wood between us.

Birds dance in erratic circles
seeking the way.
Trees provide a canopy of light—
white snow against dark.

Time melts
with each footstep.
Carrying you back to me
is the memory of trees,
soft earth buried beneath cold,
green that knows
you will be near again.
Even the seasons herald you to my door.

Crossing Invisible Lines

They first met in the dreamtime,
an open field of golden honey bales
and pine trees bordering the fence.
His tweed jacket and pocket kerchief looked odd to her.
Her thin sundress looked too modern to him.
Their meetings were brief and infrequent.

At exactly 3am, her eyes would open
and then close, eyelids fluttering until
the hum of the ceiling fan mimicked
the music of this other space.
They sat amongst dry stalks of wheat,
asking each other as many questions as possible.

If either he awakened or she awakened,
the connection between worlds would break,
and the field would dissolve.

The sudden disappearing felt like looking at the sky
through too bright rays of sun.
Flashes of white made all tangible things
lose their outline,
until even the field would fade.

Never meeting during the day,
sometimes going weeks
without a rendezvous,
time condensed on these nights.

Lovers in an unknown land
balance on this thin thread.

To Celebrate the Bountiful

(Inspired by Kohbar of Mithila, by Padma Shri Sita Devi)

My love for you is a thousand suns
with adoring eyes all circling in rotation.
My love for you is the fish that swims upstream
with only the promise of reaching you.

I paint our world bright yellows
and brave orange hues,
fingertips pigmenting the walls with color.
I pluck a golden globe from the sky,
like a dandelion in the field,
just to light the lamp of life
with tender offerings.

Joined by a bounty of threaded beads,
we are surrounded by luscious berries
falling off the vine,
a feathered crown bird,
a necklace adorned turtle,
and the young elephant draped in fine silks.

The circle of us jumps from splashes of ochre
to deep pools of tawny red.
We rise to the surface,
resplendent with feathers and blossoms.
My love for you is a celestial celebration,
a festival of the marriage of all things.

The Quiet Hum of Existence

(Inspired by an image by Jemima Muir)

Her limbs are made of lemonade.
She appears every night in my dreams
wearing circus pants to make me smile,
and watering my mind
with fertile thoughts of what is possible.
In March, we hit the pause button.
Tomorrow has become a challenging concept.
Why not dance today? She asks.
Why not walk, even if it's raining?
My sleep time godmother
keeps offering suggestions,
and I listen.

She plants seeds for me and for many.
I start to see familiar faces.
Each strident walker and avid bicyclist
has the telltale signs of someone
who hears the same whispers.
A green sprout here, a dangling leaf there,
everyone is connected by the growth of hope.
We oil our joints like the Tin Man of Oz,
by walking.
A newfound agility makes taking new steps
much easier.

Some days we start from scratch
with a new patch of earth.
Other days, we water the same rows,
clip branches, help guide the new buds
reaching for sunlight.
The secret ingredient is movement,

using one muscle at a time—
a spinning wheel,
a steady heartbeat,
the quiet hum of existence.

Leave the Light On

(Inspired by an image by Joelle Chmiel)

There are full rooms and empty rooms
and a long stairwell leading to the beginning of it all.
Concrete steps lead back up
to where we are now—
where the light sometimes shines a warm hue
of gold, or burnished red.
Other times, I am reminded of aqua waves
and an otherworldly violet.

The people come and go.
It is seldom the same collection,
and yet, the gathering always has
someone laughing
someone singing
someone crying
someone arguing
someone feeling lonely
and someone wanting to flee.

There must always be room for
empty compartments—
places only your singular heart
knows how to find.
If the rooms are always full,
too full,
the mind has nowhere to go.
There is no refuge from the noise and clamor.

Safeguard the heart.
Protect the tiny space of comfort
you reserve for reveries.
Keep the staircase well lit.

A Mind Filled with Stars

(Inspired by an image by Helen Marten)

Each day is a journey to the center of a tangerine sky.
The spark of an idea is the spiral in the storm,
our own light source energy expanding
and contracting like the heart's beating muscle.
With feet planted in the roots of a memory jar,
winged creatures appear, reminding us
of the stairs we once climbed.
We live many lives,
morph between caterpillar stages,
walking with bare feet in the soil
of past selves—
the budding artist who dares to experiment,
the brave swimmer making that first dive,
the student who raises a hand to
speak up and speak out.
An electric grid of connectivity
streams from tender feet to a mind
filled with stars.
An ink blot of indigo guides us to that
new thought emerging.
With a solar flare burst,
eyes wide with wonder,
we hold in our hands the fragile creation
meant for this day.
We cradle the gift
and marvel at the muse,
before it disappears into mystery.

We Stitch Ourselves Together

You conjure with your hands
the knitting together of days,
finding comfort in simple tasks.
Small strands of hope
have replaced every familiar note
on the piano.

We mourn the loss of normal.
We find new names for things.
We rebirth ourselves
as if planting trees.
Digging deep with unsure feet,
beckoning growth,
we find solace in building a new forest together.

Our hands look different,
more vulnerable.
Our fingers sift days
like flour.
We move more slowly,
breathing through cloth
and appreciating oxygen
like never before.
We stitch ourselves together
every morning
with threads of resilience.

A Safe Place to Breathe

(Inspired by the photography of Khadija Saye)

Courage lives in my fingers.
I hold on my lips
the whispers of my ancestors.
These things matter.
A safe place to live
and breathe,
safe walls,
safe floors,
safe ceilings—
these necessities
belong to everyone.

We house ourselves
with faith,
believing in those
who build dwellings in the sky.
With closed eyelids,
I see smoke devour that safety.
There are eyes that see what needs to be fixed,
and there are eyes that ignore the bricks out of place.
When every floor of every tower building
has unwavering strength,
our vulnerable feet will have peace.

(Note: The photographer died in the Grenfell Tower fire, London, 2017)

The No Name Time

The day's lingering perfume
leaves a vapor trail of words
and footsteps.

The lowering light through the window
slows the pulse.

Just as you slip
between cool, welcoming sheets,
the mind becomes liquid.

Small droplets of thought, like pearls,
leave a dotted line,
leading to the door of
another world.

You sink to the bottom of an ocean dream,
exchanging glances with creatures
who need no light
and conversing with jellyfish.

Limbs heavy with sleep,
your hands become transparent,
unable to touch things,
yet still part of this dimension.

You become the lead actor
in this under-the-sea adventure,
until the sun peeks through
narrow cracks in the blinds,
breaking the spell of night with day.

Closing Time

Last call for drinks,
last game of darts—
words hang in the air,
comingling with smoke
and the slowing down of time.
No muscles move to leave
this space.
Shoulder to shoulder in the booth,
we are both liquid and bone.
An energy current binds us.
Tiny explosive connections,
lightning speed thought,
a ping pong ball of ideas bounces
across the room.
The corner table mirror reflects
our eager eyes in return.
We see our own faces,
shocked by the familiar.
Is there anything new we could possibly say?
Tonight was a tornado of words.
It's closing time now.
Our hands can't even hold pens.
Every last coin of thought has been spent.
In writing circles and lecture halls,
we weave and re-weave
tomorrow's world in our heads.
But for now, it's closing time.

This Was How He Played

He gathered moonlight with his song,
brought the taste of the day
to his lips—
each note an offering
to ancestors.

His hands danced along the keys.
The choreography of melody
told a story,
and we listened for clues.
Lush tunes with augmented chords,
he used the pedal with purpose
to let notes linger.

The confines of his day at the bank
were abandoned for music.
His commute home, now long forgotten.
His hurried lunch,
replaced by a languorous supper.

This was how my grandfather played the piano.

Body Rhythms

The sound of the beat
hits the tip of my tongue,
reverberating through the body.
Sound travels.
A trumpet blare opens my lungs.
Smooth and sweet,
the bass line slips
into the bloodstream.
A glissando and a glide,
I ride through the music.
Notes punching the night air
with a staccato syncopation—
musical punctuation.
The head roars,
a siren sound.
The room has moving parts,
so I spin with the hum
and hum with the spin.

We Breathe the Same Air

(Inspired by an image by Omid Armin)

My lungs fill and fly with the wind.
My heart is this fast-moving cloud.
With root chakra energy,
I step into the daylight,
unsure of the welcoming I long for.
I thought this land promised
open arms.

In a newfound place to call home,
I pull my coat tighter,
every button secure.
Holding a bag of hope,
I look out at the open space
of possibility.
The pavement I walk on
is streaked with burnt orange.
The sky above
is a cornflower blue.
The sound of beeping horns
does not hamper my ability
to see what could be.

We breathe the same air—
shop at the same stores.
We scramble eggs in a skillet—
serve them up to our hungry families.
My children,
your children,
they are all just children.
We are all just human.

The Last Drop of Water

(Inspired by Orlando (Legs) by Valérie Mannaerts)

To touch the leg that dances across the universe,
to feel the pulse of a thousand suns shining—
this—
this is where we must live.
We create and re-create our world.

The curve of my knee is irrelevant.
Can you see inside my veins?
Can you see into the heart of each word,
waiting to drip onto the page,
like a Dali painting?

Our only hope is connection.
I see the sculpture of your youth
and notice the fleeting beauty,
which we all possess in early years.
What I want to understand
are the less traveled cells,
where the truth of who you are
sings the highest note without shame
or regret.
You are the light touch of dawn
when the shadows flee.
You are the last drop of water
on this earth.

Breathing Peace

If peace was something we could hold
in our hands,
we would mold it like clay.
We would shape it into a circle,
leaving our thumbprint on it,
then carefully pass it into
the knowing hands of the next person,
as if handling a newborn sparrow.

If peace was something we could breathe,
we would close our eyes and savor the precious air
flowing into our lungs—
passing through our lips.
That exhale would be a prayer.
It would be a song in three-part harmony.

If peace was something we could taste,
it would be figs drizzled with honey.
We would arrange it on a plate
with a silk-petaled sunflower
decorating the center.
We would pass the plate around
with reverence, ensuring that every single person
received nourishment.

If peace was something we could walk to,
it would be a sacred labyrinth of circles.
We would greet each other on the meditative path.
We would come together at the center
and admire our cohesive union—
arms raised to the sun,
rejoicing in what we could not see or touch,
but we could feel it.

We have been walking together
for such a long time.
We have always been at peace,
but we become lost in the forgetting.

About the Author

Cristina M. R. Norcross lives in Wisconsin and is the author of 8 poetry collections. She is the founding editor of *Blue Heron Review*. Her latest book is *Beauty in the Broken Places* (Kelsay Books, 2019). Cristina's other recent collections include *Amnesia and Awakenings* (Local Gems Press, 2016) and *Still Life Stories* (Kelsay Books, 2016). One of her poems from *Beauty in the Broken Places* was nominated for a Pushcart Prize. Cristina's poems have been published widely in online and print journals including: *Visual Verse, Your Daily Poem, Right Hand Pointing, Verse-Virtual, The Ekphrastic Review, Poetry Hall, Bramble, As Above So Below,* and *Pirene's Fountain,* among others. Her work has also been published in numerous print anthologies, including most recently, *Through This Door: Wisconsin in Poems* (Art Night Books, 2020) and *Floored* (Kingly Street Press, 2021). She has helped organize community art and poetry projects, has led writing workshops, and has also hosted many open mic poetry readings. Cristina hosts an online writing prompt group on Facebook called, Connection and Creativity During Challenging Times. She was a featured poet and is a regular, contributing poet for the online series, WNP Virtual Open Mic, Poetry Through the Pandemic, with host Kai Coggin. Cristina is one of the co-founders of Random Acts of Poetry and Art Day (celebrated annually on February 20th). Find out more about this author: www.cristinanorcross.com

Made in the USA
Las Vegas, NV
31 March 2024

88014910R00028